This Little Bird

This little bird flaps its wings.

blue tit

QED ESSENTIALS

Let's Read

This Little Bird

Sasha Morton

Quarto is the authority on a wide range of topics.

Quarto educates, entertains and enriches the lives of our readers—enthusiasts and lovers of hands-on living.

www.quartoknows.com

Author: Sasha Morton
Series Editor: Joyce Bentley
Consultant: Helen Marron
Designer: Elaine Wilkinson

© 2019 Quarto Publishing plc

First published in 2019 by QED Publishing,
an imprint of The Quarto Group.
The Old Brewery, 6 Blundell Street,
London N7 9BH, United Kingdom.
T (0)20 7700 6700 F (0)20 7700 8066
www.QuartoKnows.com

MIX
Paper from responsible sources
FSC® C001701

Manufactured in Shenzhen, China PP072019

9 8 7 6 5 4 3 2 1

A catalogue record for this book is available from the British Library.

ISBN 978-0-7112-4412-2

Photo Acknowledgments
Shutterstock: front cover PrakapenkaAlena; back cover and p2 clarst5; title page, p19 and 22 Ondrej Prosicky; p3 and 10-11 PrakapenkaAlena; p4-5 Victor Tyakht; p5 hfuchs; p6t taviphoto; p6b taviphoto; p7 Kletr; p8 YK; p9 Vishnevskiy Vasily; p12 and 20 Petr Salinger; p13 and 20 Henderbeth; p14t zokru; p14b Susanna Hietanen; p15 and 20 Tom Middleton; p16, 20 and 22 snomedia; p16-17 gabrisigno; p18 and 23 ploypemuk; p18l Super Prin; p21 Gelpi

It has some blue feathers and some yellow feathers.

This little bird gets food from a shell.

This little bird gets food from a feeder.

nuts

This bird feeds the little bird in a tree!

7

The blackbird eggs in this nest are blue.

8

The blackbird feeds the little blackbirds.

9

Three little birds sit on a twig.

budgie

They have little beaks and long claws.

beak

claws

11

Some birds have big beaks.

toucan

Some birds have big feathers.

peacock

This little bird sits
in the snow.
It is a robin.

This blue tit sits
near a bird box
in the snow.

This big bird is an owl.

This bird is a puffin.

Puffins have nests near the sea.

Birds can have red, blue and yellow feathers.

parrot

This green bird is a parakeet.

Tweet! Tweet!

19

Your Turn

Match it!
Follow the line from each picture
to read the word.

owl

toucan

puffin

peacock

parakeet

Clap it!

Say the 'Match it!' words.
Clap and count
the syllables.

Sound it!

Sound out each of these words.

f oo d   t w i g   n e s t   w i ng

Say it!

Read and say these words.

some   have   little   you   they

Spot it!

1. **Look at page 6.** Which word begins with **sh**?

2. **Look at page 11.** Which word ends with **ng**?

Finish it!

Look back and find which word is missing.

1. **Page 12.** Some birds have big _____ .

2. **Page 17.** Puffins have _____ near the sea.

Count it!

1. **Page 5.** How many times does the word **some** appear?

2. **Page 18.** How many times does the word **and** appear?

Answers: **Spot it!** 1 shell 2 long
Finish it! 1 beaks 2 nests **Count it!** 1 two 2 one

Sort it!

Sort the letters to spell a word.
Can you find the word in the book?

1 n i r o b

2 e ll sh

3 g ee n r

4 a l f p

Do it!

Draw one of the birds from the book.
Label the wings, feathers,
beak and claws.

Notes for Parents and Teachers

Children naturally practise their literacy skills as they discover the world around them. The topics in the **QED Essentials** series help children use these developing skills and broaden their knowledge and vocabulary. Once they have finished reading the text, encourage your child to demonstrate their understanding by having a go at the activities on pages 20–23.

Reading Tips

• Sit next to your child and let them turn the pages themselves.

• Look through the book before you start reading together. Discuss what you can see on the cover first.

• Encourage your child to use a finger to track the text as they read.

• Keep reading and talking sessions short and at a time that works for both of you. Try to make it a relaxing moment to share with your child.

• Prompt your child to use the picture clues to support their reading when they come across unfamiliar words.

• Give lots of praise as your child reads and return to the book as often as you can. Re-reading leads to greater confidence and fluency.

• Remind your child to use their letter sound knowledge to work out new words.

• Use the 'Your Turn' pages to practise reading new words and to encourage your child to talk about the text.

Colourful photographs open up further discussion points

Birds can have red, blue and yellow feathers.

parrot

Wide range of vocabulary to explore in context

This green bird is a parakeet.

Tweet! Tweet!

Short, decodable sentences repeat topic words and commonly used words

18

19